Trog and the dog

GW01393000

by Ben Butterworth
pictures by Lorraine Calaora

Nelson

Trog was tired.
Father was tired.
Grandpa Gripe was very tired.
They had run after the sheep
for hours.

'We shall never get them
into the fold,' Father said.
'I'm going home.'

'I'm going home,' Trog said.

'I'm going to bed,' said Grandpa.

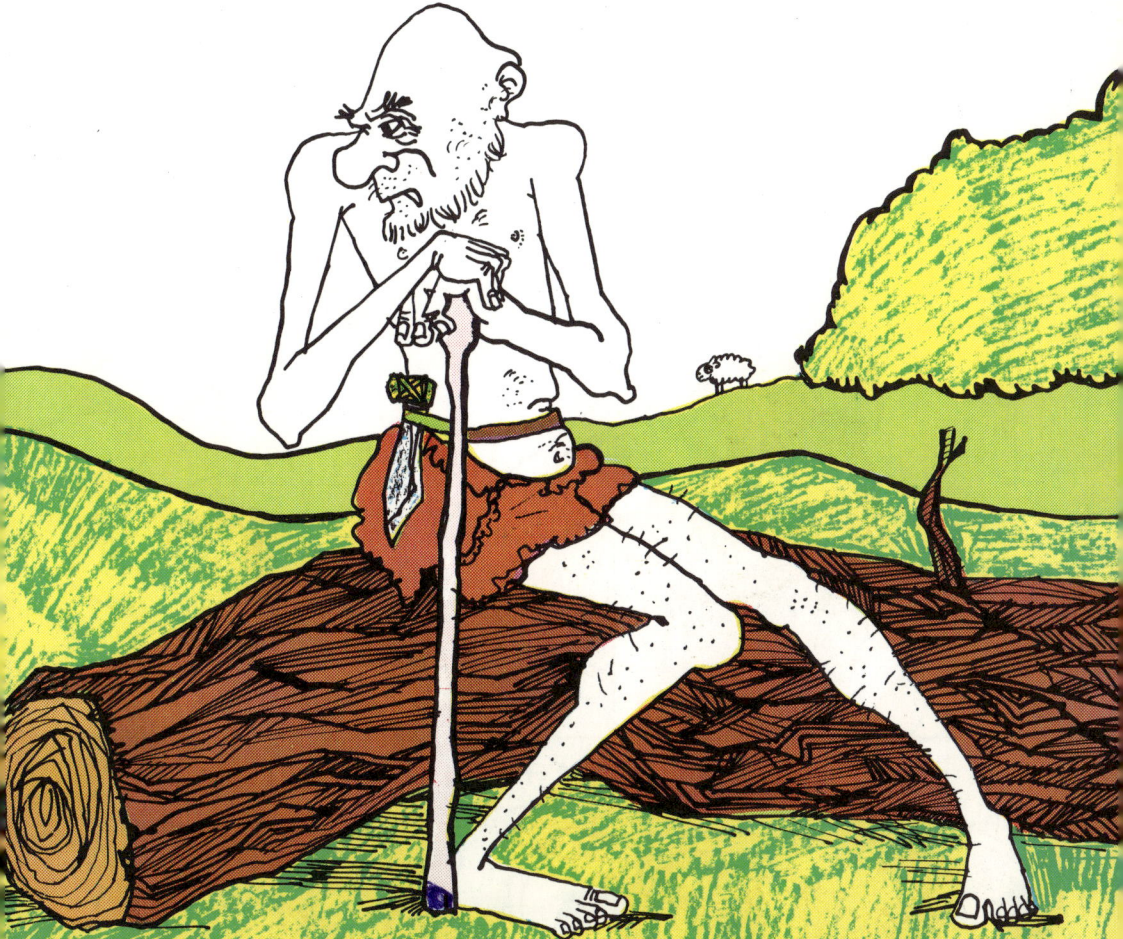

'The Quickerwits
do not run after the sheep all day,'
Mother said to them.
'They get the sheep into the fold
very quickly.
Go and see how they do it.'

'I will go,' said Grandpa Gripe.

Grandpa went over the hills,
over the rivers,
to the land of the Quickerwits.

'Now,' Grandpa said,
'how do you get the sheep in?
We have to run after them
for hours.'

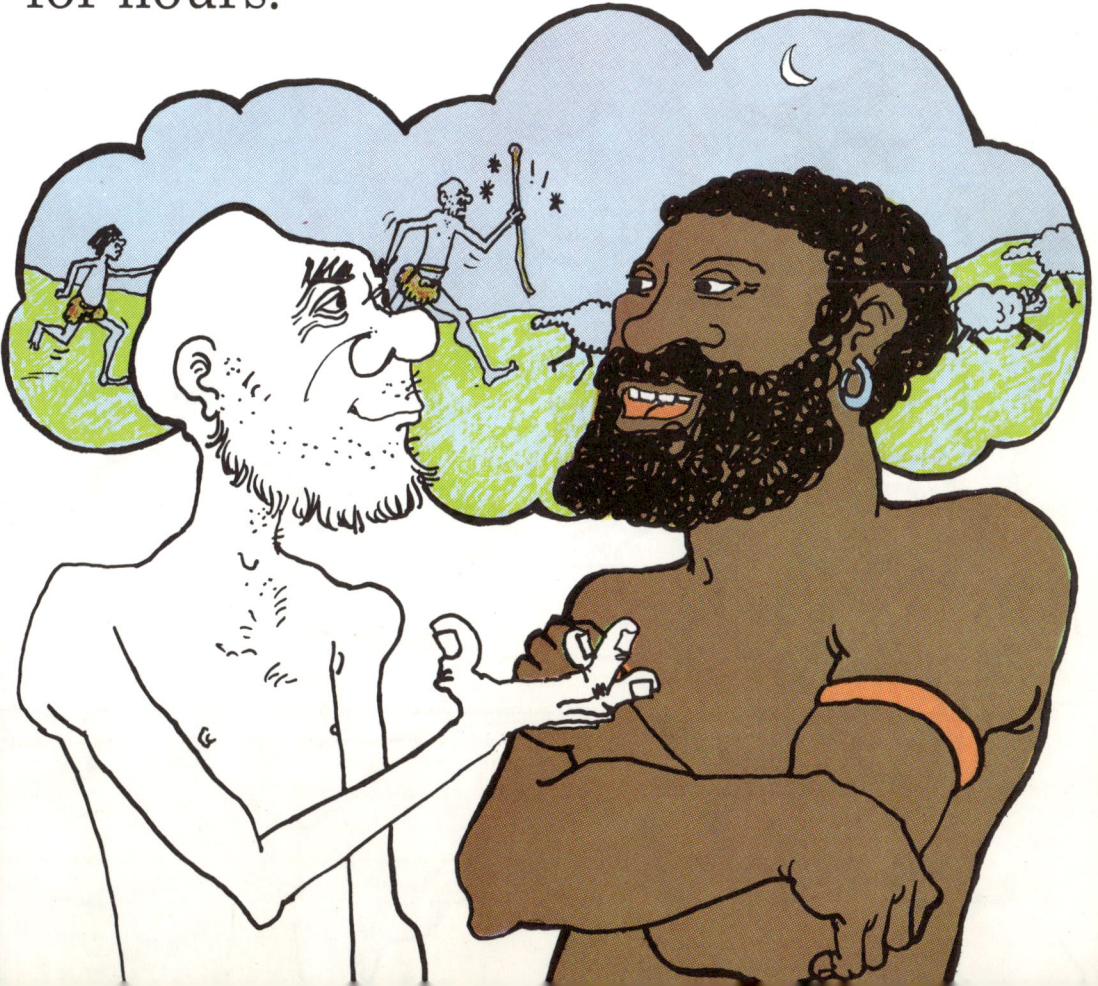

'It's easy,' the Quickerwits said.
'It's very easy.
We don't run after the sheep at all.
We train a dog.
The dog gets the sheep for us.

We find a baby wolf and train it.
For one whistle
he runs round the back of the sheep.
For two whistles
he runs round the front.
For three whistles he sits still.
He soon gets the sheep in.'

Grandpa went back
to Father and Trog.

'It's easy,' Grandpa said.
'The Quickerwits train a dog.
The dog runs
after the sheep for you.
All you have to do is to whistle.
I will train one.'

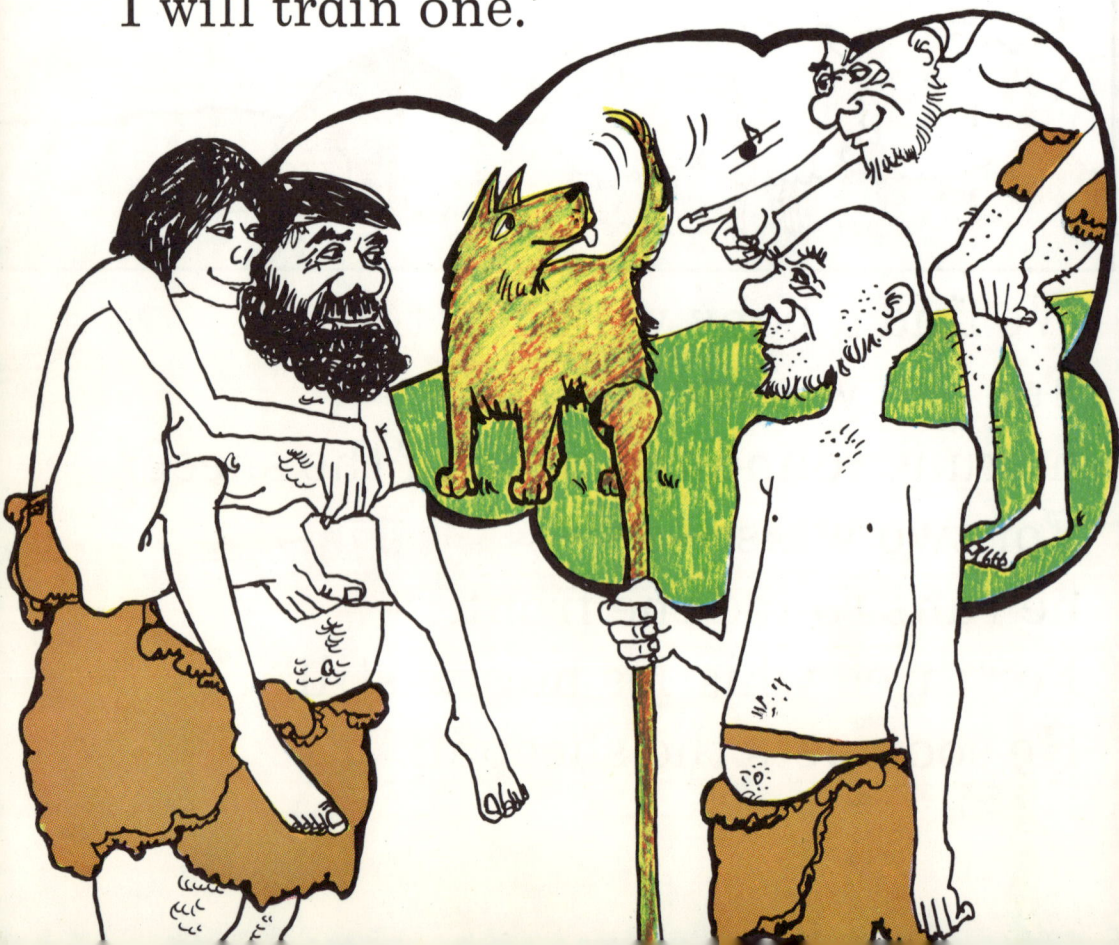

Grandpa found a baby wolf.
He began to train it.
It bit his finger.
It bit his hand.
It bit him on the leg.
It bit him so often
that he called it Snap.

One day
Grandpa said, 'Snap is trained now.'

He went away with the dog
and soon came back.

'The sheep are all in,' he said.
'It's easy
when you have Snap with you.'

The next night
Father went with Snap.
He came back in no time at all.

'All the sheep are in,' he said.
'Trog is going next.'

The next night Trog went with Snap.

'Now then,' Trog said, 'let's see . . .
One whistle,
that's for round the back.
No, it's for round the front.
No, that's three whistles.
No, it's four.'
Trog gave one, two, three whistles,
and then three, two, one whistles.

Snap ran here.

The sheep ran there.

Trog ran,
Snap ran,
the sheep ran.

Snap was tired of Trog
and his whistling.

14

Then Trog gave four whistles
and Snap ran away.
So did the sheep.

Trog went home.

'Now,' Grandpa asked,
'are all the sheep in the fold?'

'No, I lost them,' Trog said.

'And where is my dog?'
asked Grandpa.

'I lost Snap too,' Trog said.

'**You lost my dog!**'
shouted Grandpa Gripe.
'That dog bit my finger.
He bit my hand.
He bit my leg.
But I trained him—
and now you have lost him.
You can train the next one.
And I hope it bites you too!'